Department of language Sciences Ca' Foscari University, Venice

Paolo E. Balboni

Intercultural Communicative Competence: A Model

Guerra Edizioni

Documents in Language Teaching Methodology
General editor: Prof. Paolo E. Balboni

A publication of "Laboratorio ITALS – Teaching Italian to Speakers of Other Languages" within the Department of Language Sciences, Ca' Foscari University, Venice.

Title: Intercultural Communicative Competence: A Model
Author: Paolo E. Balboni
English translation: David Newbold
Publication No. 2 in the series
Year of Publication: 2006
© Copyright 2006, Guerra Edizioni, Via A. Manna, 25
06132 Perugia

ISBN 978-88-7715-926-7

Finito di stampare nel mese di agosto 2006 da Guerra guru srl - Perugia

Table of contents

1. Stating the problem

The literature on intercultural communicative competence (hence: ICCC) has been growing steadily since the late 1980s, following the increasing use of English as a *lingua franca* and the growing awareness that English might be able to resolve a specific communication problem but it could not provide a basis for real communication.

Most of the literature concerns either international management and trade, or migrant integration and EU intercultural policies. Very few studies focus on the semiotics of ICCC and on the problem of ICCC in the acquisition and learning of second and foreign languages.

In recent years there has been an increasing interest in ICCC. *per se* and in the problems of acquiring/teaching ICCC, both in schools and, especially, in companies, where intercultural communication is a daily problem, and where personnel find themselves working within a context of life-long learning: the activity of the Council of Europe has played a major role in this process, mainly through the work of such scholars as Byram, Zarate, Béacco (Byram, Zarate 1996; Byram 1997; Byram, Béacco 2003).

Most of the research available is *descriptive*, which is only natural in the pioneer phase of ICCC studies. In our opinion, however, the descriptive perspective is a starting point but it is not enough from the theoretical point of view. A shift from *description* to *modelling* is needed, in order to design a process of *competence building*, because descriptions cannot be taught (or are useless if they are taught), while models can be taught and competences, based on models, developed (cf 2.2.2).

The approach of the Venice school of LTM normally begins with the definition of an epistemological model, i.e. with the analysis of a type of knowledge which underlies a phenomenon. This is the subject of the first section in this chapter.

1.1 An epistemological framework

As we have just said, the descriptive approach has to evolve into a model, if a curriculum for developing ICCC is to be designed. Let us look more closely at the terms used in this statement.

1.1.1 *Model and Competence*

We first have to refer to four fundamental 'declarations' (the concept of 'declarative knowledge' will be studied in 1.1.4).

a. First declaration

> *By 'model' we mean a generative framework, i.e. a pattern or a structure which can include all possible occurrences, and is able to generate behaviour.*

Or, in more familiar terms: a model such as communicative *competence* is of no use if it does not generate communicative *performance*.
This statement is at the heart of the Modern Language Projects and the *Common European Framework* which the Council of Europe has been working on for the last four decades. (We shall return to the nature of models in the second chapter).

b. Second declaration

> Models are often internally structured in a hierarchical manner.

This means that a model may consist of a group of lower level models, which are low level when used in that specific pattern, but can be high level models when used *per se*. For example, 'language competence' is a high level model when it declares that to know a language means to know four grammars (phonology/graphemics, morpho/syntax, lexicon, textuality), but a secondary model when inserted into a higher ranking model such as 'communicative competence.'
Let us consider the hierarchical structure of the models we are beginning to work on:

> - *Language competence* in English (to refer to a specific language) is a model which derives from a number of interacting sub-models which make up what is usually called 'English grammar'. This competence generates validation or falsification of correctness ("you have an apple" is a true

English sentence, "you an apple have" is not, since English syntax does not include the possibility of an object preceding the verb; but this latter sequence is possible in Italian and compulsory in Japanese);

- *Communicative competence* in English is higher in level than mere *language competence* as it also includes sociolinguistic, pragmalinguistics, and extralinguistic grammars. Through the interaction of these grammars *communicative competence* in English generates comprehension, production, and interaction in this language;

- *Intercultural communicative competence* is a still higher level model, as it cannot be followed by a specification such as "in English", as in point (b) above. At least two languages/cultures are to be specified, e.g., "ICCC of Spaniards and Turks". ICCC. is a complex model which comes from a comparison between at least two communicative competences in two languages and cultures in order to allow interaction between the two.

c. Third declaration

The higher the level of a model, the greater its complexity - but the complexity of a model, does not necessarily lead to complexity in extensio, but rather in profundis.

A useful example of this declaration (which we shall return to in chapter 2) is a website homepage, which may have three or four hot words, each of them opening in depth onto other pages, followed by other in-depth expansions and so on. These links add complexity to the simple appearance of the homepage.

The ICCC we are describing here is an *in profundis* hypertext, very simple in its surface form, and thus very easy to handle, but which aims at describing/generating all possible IC communicative exchanges in all possible communicative events.

d. Fourth declaration

Models are forms of declarative knowledge which must generate procedural knowledge

In cognitive sciences there are two fundamental forms of knowledge:

- declarations: these usually contain two parts linked by a verb (*be, have, are composed of, is equal to,* etc.). For example, "all the languages of the world have at least three functions: subject, verb, object". This declaration, which like all declarative knowledge is simple, can be applied to all human languages and *generates* a series of secondary declarations, or corollaries (for example: "there are six possible sequences of the three elements present in every language: SVO, SOV, OSV, OVS, VSO, VOS") and also applications for specific situations (for example: "in English and French the standard sequence is SVO, while Hebrew and Arabic use VSO, and Hindi and Turkish use SOV", and so on);

- procedures: declarations can be easily taught, but are useless unless they become – once again in the terms of cognitive sciences – *procedural knowledge* based on "if... then...". The declaration about sequence, above, generates this procedure: "*If* the standard sequence in English is SVO, *then* I must say *this is an apple* and not *an apple this is* ...": (This idea of grammar as 'model' derives from Langacker 1990).

To conclude we can thus 'declare' that:

models are a form of declarative knowledge about something, where only relevant features emerge (see point 3) and the rest is not ignored but set on lower levels, like branches in Chomskyan tree diagrams that can be explored with a top down logic.	a *model becomes a competence when it is able to generate behaviour:* this occurs when the model is applied to a context of *performance.*
↓	↓
a *model may be taught, since it is a form of knowledge which can be transmitted:* a teacher can write a rule on the blackboard or can help the students to discover it.	*competence cannot be taught,* but must be constructed, filling in the elements of the model with the information, declarations and procedures to be used in the performance phase.

Since ICCC is a *competence*, it cannot be taught. Yet, once a reliable *model* of it has been provided, it can be built up.

Once the model is there, it can be either applied to simple contexts, e.g. "ICCC between Germans and Turks" or to more complex contexts, typical of globalized society, e.g. "ICCC between people involved in an international military mission and interacting in English as a lingua franca".

1.1.2 *Economy* and *reliability* as qualities of efficient models

In order to work, a model needs to be economic in structure and reliable in contents.

a. *Economy*
A model must be *economic*, i.e. *easy to remember and use.*
Some facts can be explained by simple models: e.g., "learning can be motivated by need, obligation or pleasure". This threefold model is powerful enough to describe all learning in all places at all times – and its pedagogical consequences are enormous: for example, we can analyze a syllabus, a teaching unit, or a lesson through this model and find what type of motivation, if any, it activates, and how to increase motivation.
In order to be economic to use a model must be *simple*. Simplicity is necessary at the surface level of a model, complexity can be added by working in depth, as in the example of the website homepage above (1.1.1.c).
To learn a model does not mean to learn each in depth sub-heading by heart, but to become able to re-construct it in any given context since one understands the logic which governs the model. You do not learn a model, but the logic underlying it.

b. *Reliability*
For a model to be *reliable*, the information it contains must be true.
It is possible to have a reliable ICCC model, while it is not possible to have a reliable description of ICCC. Intercultural communication changes continuously under the pressure of worldwide mass media (mostly American and Indian) and of interpersonal contacts which are a result of the process of globalization. The latter term usually refers to economics, trade, science, and the labour force – but there is also a globalization of communicative models, both at surface level (e.g. shaking hands, etc.) and at a deeper level (text structuring, for example, is shifting massively towards an English -particularly American English - style; see 3.1 below).

1.1.3 *Consequences of the epistemological framework*

The dynamic and continuing evolution of intercultural communication means that ICCC is a learning process which not only lasts a lifetime, but also includes all situations and contexts in which we have to interact (in the terms of the Lisbon agreement, *lifelong and lifewide learning*). As a consequence,

> *rather than teaching IC.C.C. we should teach a model for lifelong observation of communication among people belonging to different cultures, so that the data can be updated and remain reliable over time.*

In the second chapter we shall try to give a *model for observing intercultural communication,* pointing out the critical points where conflict may arise, so that each person may be able to adjourn his or her intercultural communication proficiency with the information he or she gathers through experience, mass media, reading, anecdotes told by colleagues, and so on.

1.1.4 *Synthesis*

The key words in this chapter are:

a.   model → competence
b.   teaching (a model) → constructing (a competence)
c.   economy of a model: simple at surface level, in depth complexity
d.   reliability: a model can be reliable, whereas the competence based on a model must be continuously validated and reshaped

2. A model of ICCC

As we have already seen, a model must be simple: to use Legrenzi's (2002, p. 56-61) words, a model is a software which includes all and only the relevant features of an idea, of an action, of an object, which are independent from the hardware used to actually implement them.

Only the emerging properties of the object must be presented in a model, so that it is not blurred or loaded with irrelevant secondary information; to understand this concept better, we could take the analogy of a scale model of a building constructed by architects to give an idea of the use of space, but from which the windows and doors, etc., have been omitted so that the focus remains on what is essential. This concept is simply an application of the fundamental rule in the theory of communication: "providing more information means informing less".

2.1 A formal model of ICCC

As a consequence of this principle, the model of ICCC we are proposing includes only three components, three "headings", which we can describe by using the metaphor of software, following Hofstede (1991):

a. *the software of the mind*
This refers to the cultural factors which affect communication.
We have to be wary of the definition which we have just given: we are not interested in *all* cultural factors (although these might interest scholars interested in intercultural pedagogy, European citizenship, models of integration for immigrants, etc.) but only those factors which affect communication, i.e. the exchange of messages between two or more people who are pursuing specific goals through communicating with others.
This software, to continue the metaphor, works like the system files inside a computer: the user is unaware of them until a warning that there is a problem appears on the screen; similarly, we are unaware of the existence of many *cultural* values, which usually seem perfectly *natural* to us, and therefore shared by all potential interlocutors;

b. *the communication software*
This refers to the codes in use, both verbal and non verbal.
The main problem here is that all our attention is directed towards verbal language, the choice of words and their morpho-syntactic organisation, while no attention is paid to non-verbal body language (gestures, expressions, proximity of speakers to each other, smells, noises), since this is imagined to be universal, and little attention is paid to the language of body ornaments such as clothes, jewels, etc.;

c. *the context software*
This is the socio-pragmatic software which governs the beginning, the direction, and the conclusion
of a communicative event (whether monocultural or intercultural). We are using the term
'communicative event' as defined in the ethnomethodology of communication, and particularly by
Dell Hymes (1972).

The first two sets of 'softwares' - cultural and communicative - constitute *competence*, while the third, the 'context software' makes it possible to move from competence to *performance*.
In visual terms, this model of ICCC can be revealed in all its simplicity in the diagramme.

The diagram should be interpreted as follows:

Intercultural communication is governed by competence groups, respectively verbal and non-verbal, and is realised in the context of communicative events governed by grammars which contain both universal elements and local cultural elements.

The icons used for the three sets of grammars (verbal, non-verbal, contextual) are meant to suggest the in-depth construction of the model, (see 1.1.1), which maintains an extremely simple and flexible surface structure.

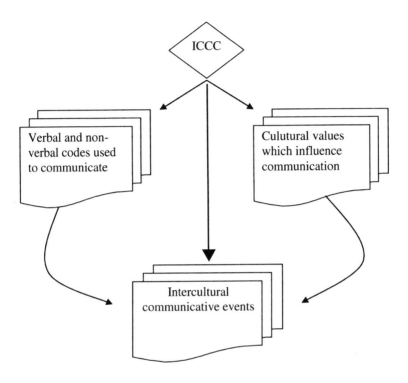

We shall now see the relevant features of each of the three components but we suggest – for the sake of efficiency – to further develop the model above by splitting the code icon into two icons, separating the linguistic codes from the non-verbal codes, as this makes the whole model easier to handle without making it any less economic (see p. 16).

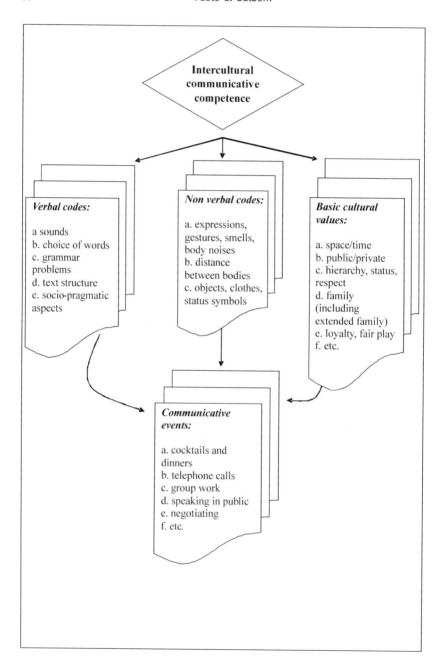

2.2 Open sets and closed systems in a model of ICCC

In Halliday's words, model are of two types: *closed system*, i.e., no further elements can of need be added, and *open sets*, which can always be modified. For example, personal pronouns form a *closed system,* while the lexicon is an *open set.*
In the diagram above the grammars belonging to ICCC belong to both types:

> a. the icons for verbal and non-verbal codes refer to closed systems. This means that all grammars of all languages are described by these headings;
> b. the icons for cultural values and communicative events, which conclude *etc.,* refer to open sets, which can always be updated and/or integrated, to suit the requirements of an individual, a group, or a society.

In other words: no user of the model can decide to exclude phonology from the "verbal code component", because a verbal code, i.e. a language, is a closed system made up of phonological, morpho-syntactical, lexical, textual and socio-pragmatic components; in contrast, the list of relevant cultural values or contexts can be modified at any time.
This difference explains the different treatment afforded the four icons in the chapters which follow, and in which they are described in more detail.

2.3 The generative power of the model

So far we have discussed the formal and logical nature of the model.
But in defining "model" we pointed out that this must be generative; it must help generate behaviour. To do so, users (and teachers) of this model of ICCC must continue to add to the contents of the four icons on the basis of their experience of life, the films they see, the anecdotes they hear - and the books they study to learn more about ICCC.
In the chapters which follow we shall map these four icons and indicate the main communicative problems; the list is not meant to be exhaustive, but rather, an exemplification.

2.4 Synthesis

The key words of this chapter are:

a. software of the mind, communication software, context software
b. open sets vs closed systems

3. Verbal codes

a. textuality
b. lexicon
c. morphosyntax
d. phonology
e. socio-pragmatics

To use De Saussure's dichotomy, a language may be viewed as *langue*, the language system, and *parole*, the system when in use and which produces social effects.

When observing and describing *langue* to identify those elements to be listed in the icon, we find four levels: textuality; the lexicon; morphology and syntax (we do not think a further division is necessary here); and phonology.

If we add the Saussurian concept of *parole*, another relevant factor emerges, i.e. pragmatics.

Each of these levels contains elements which can be a source of IC conflict, making communication difficult or preventing it from taking place.

These five elements are fundamental in a description of ICCC.

3.1 Critical points in textuality

A text (whether written, oral, or multimedial, is irrelevant) produced by an English or an American speaker tends to go straight to the point through a series of very simple juxtaposed segments:

Each segment, i.e., each sentence in English, tends to be made up of subject and verb, plus object, time, space, condition complements as needed.

In contrast, a text produced by a Romance speaker or by a German speaker, tends to fuse all the segments, the arrows above, into a more complex sentence: this is possible because Romance and German personal pronouns include gender and number and verbs have many marked forms, so the textual structure which can be built up is by far more complex than the texture allowed by English where the pronoun *it* might often refer to many previous nouns and the verbal system only differentiates the third person singular. This makes it more difficult to create links between one sentence and the next - something which is far easier in Italian, Spanish, German.

In technical terms, English makes use of *parataxis* (coordination between sentences) while Romance languages and German use *hypotaxis*, or subordinate clauses. As a result, errors may be made in each direction by an interlocutor:

a. Europeans vs. Americans
an Italian may consider an English text to be banal or superficial because it uses very simple sentences, such as might be used by children at primary school: e.g., a text by Hemingway is banal, a project looks like a shopping list, and so on;

b. Americans vs. Europeans
an American (or the speaker of an oriental language who has studied English in America, and for whom English is the first Indo-European language) may consider a text in German to be ambiguous and waffling, as if the speaker were trying to hide something...

c. Europeans and Americans vs. Asians
Both English, Romance and German speakers have problems with Oriental texts, which can be viewed as a spiral which slowly proceeds from the distant outskirts of the matter discussed to the heart of the matter, creating the impression, for the American or European listener, that they are being 'taken for a ride'. In contrast, a Chinese or Japanese speaker, an Indian or an Arab may consider it extremely rude to go straight to the point.

Text construction is a critical point of ICCC because *we are unaware of our text building strategies and when using English as a lingua franca, each speaker tends to construct a text following the mechanisms he or she is familiar with.*

'Unaware' is a key factor: we are unaware of the strategies we use to construct a text and we apply them automatically. It may not be possible to change these strategies, but someone with good ICCC is *aware* of the problem and so does not apply preconceptions, and respects the conceptual and textual rules of the interlocutor.

3.2 Critical points in the lexicon

When we speak a foreign language - and this includes English as a lingua franca - we are particularly careful about the lexis. This is paradoxical, since it is the aspect which creates fewest intercultural problems, with the exception of two areas, the use of English words of Latin origin and of expressive words.

a. English words of Latin origin
Around 54% of the lexicon in English is of Latin origin, but for many of these words there is a Germanic equivalent; words of Latin origin tend to belong to a formal register, while Germanic words have an earthier, more informal feel. The speaker of a Romance language thus runs the risk of appearing superior and formal, while a native speaker of English may be difficult to understand, appearing to be a careless speaker determined not to help the listener understand. In Hymes' model of the communicative event, it is the psychological key which is badly interpreted, and which profoundly affects the attitude of the interlocutors.

b. Expressive words
The second problem concerns the choice of expressive words, used to colour a conversation, to understate, or to be ironic.
These words often have sexual connotations, taboo words in many cultures, which may end up transforming an intentionally ironic phrase into an insult.

3.3 Critical points in morpho-syntax

This is another aspect of language use which non-native speakers worry about, but which has few intercultural consequences. Problems can arise from the use of negative and interrogative forms, on the use of the future and with comparatives and superlatives.

3.3.1 Interrogatives

In many formal cultures based on respect there are questions which are asked simply to receive an affirmative answer, and with it, confirmation of one's social role. For example, a simple question such as "Is this the road to Nairobi?" is a neutral question for a European, but in a Swahili context it can only receive a "yes" answer – even though the road in question may not lead to Nairobi – because yes-no questions in Swahili cultures are used to state one's position and can only be answered "yes". (The question to ask is "Which is the road to Nairobi?")
A similar response occurs in Europe or America for such questions as "Can I have a glass of water?" or "Can I use the bathroom, please?": respect for a guest obliges the host to answer "yes", as a Swahili speaker will do with a foreigner, to show respect.
People with experience of working in Asia know that a European technician who asks the Chinese workman "Do you understand?" will always get the reply "yes"; to answer "no" would be to show disrespect towards the foreign 'boss', as though he were incapable of explaining himself; for the same reason of respect, if a European exporter asks his Japanese colleague in Tokyo "Do you agree?" he may receive a slight smile as an answer, and interpret it as a "yes", although the real meaning is "no"; the Japanese speaker avoids an explicit negative (a silent smile is preferred) because he or she doesn't wish to show disrespect – with devastating consequences in a negotiation situation.

3.3.2. Negatives

Different cultures give different values to dissenting.
An Italian, an Eastern European, or an Israeli will often point out the 10% of the interlocutor's words he or she disagrees with and will say

nothing about the 90% he or she agrees with. As a result, they souns aggressive to an American, who prefers to say *yes, but...* and first refers to what unites the two speakers before moving on to talk about what they do not agree about.

Similarly, many non-English speakers do not grasp the strong negation of *I'm afraid this is not possible*, in which the initial *I'm afraid* may be interpreted as a possibility, a non-final personal consideration, whereas the phrase is actually a total negation: *It isn't possible*.

3.3.3 *The future*

During the (first) Gulf War, Iraqi television continuously transmitted, with Arab subtitles, the ultimatum of President Bush Sr, which contained a series of verbs in the future, describing what would happen to Iraq if Saddam Hussein did not withdraw from Kuwait. In this way the population could hear the American's blasphemy, since he was referring to the future as if he were God.

In Arabic the future tense is reserved for the Koran, and if a speaker has to refer to the future he does so by using the present tense, an adverbial of time, and the invocation *Insh Allah* - familiar to southern Italians (*se dio vuole*) and Spanish speakers (*se dios quiere*), an inheritance, perhaps, from past centuries of Arab domination.

3.3.4 *Comparatives and superlatives*

In a Romance language to say "Pablo is *shorter* (or *less efficient*) than Pedro" has no specific connotation, whereas in English, out of politeness, "Paul is *not as tall as* (or *less efficient than*) Peter" is preferred, eliminating the *less*, or the negative connotations of a word like *short*. When it comes to superlatives, it is American English which (to European ears) seems exaggerated, since Europeans prefer understatement, and the use of superlatives may seem like boasting, and lead to a negative, even ridiculous, image of the American speaker.

An illustration of this can be seen in a common event, namely the presentation of a foreign guest or lecturer. The American will introduce the guest with a series of extremely positive remarks concerning his or her CV, experiences and achievements; these remarks are likely to prove embarrassing, if not ridiculous, to the European ear. In contrast, a simple introduction by a European host may seem too brief and sterile, even provocatively so, for the American guest.

3.4 Critical points in phonology

A language is made up of sounds, and problems related to this dimension are critical. They concern two aspects: volume, and speaking at the same time.

3.4.1 Volume

An English colleague of ours once commented that "Italians and Spaniards always quarrel, even when they agree" – but the fact is that these peoples have a loud tone of voice and that Italian and Spanish, as well as other languages such as Greek and Slav languages, being crowded with vowels, are noisier than English and Oriental languages. This intercultural problem begins when

- *unconsciously* the Englishman feels 'attacked' by the Italian's tone of voice (and this impression may be aggravated by the Italian's proximity and use of gestures, their way of drawing attention to divisions, cf. 3.3.2, and of speaking at the same time cf. 4.2);
- *unconsciously* the Italian considers the Englishman cold, distant or unfriendly because he is 'muttering' his ideas almost to himself.

The IC problem lies in the word in italics, above, rather than in the difference between English and Italians.

3.4.2 Speaking at the same time

A typical English conversation – i.e. in the lingua franca of the globalised world – is made up of a series of segments, with each speaker waiting for the interlocutor to finish before intervening:

Latin peoples tend to be more co-operative in conversation, as if they were constructing it together: as soon as the listener has understood what the other person wants to say, he or she stops them, since to go on speaking would be a waste of time, and moves on to the reply:

Although this strategy is more efficient than the English way, it is perceived as aggressive.

This sensation of aggression increases for Asians, especially from the Far East, who not only wait for the interlocutor to finish, but also wait for a second or two before replying, as if they wish to draw attention to the complexity of what has just been said, and their own desire to digest it properly.

On this topic a metaphor used by Gannon (1994) is helpful. In his book on managerial IC he describes Italians as singers in an opera house, where everyone is trying to cover the other person's voice, and where two, three or even four people are singing at the same time, and yet 'miraculously, Italians understand each other.'

3.5 Critical points in pragmatics

In previous chapters we have used the term 'socio-pragmatics' to combine the sociolinguistic and pragmatic dimensions.

The socio-linguistic dimension of register is undoubtedly important, but with English it does not create particular problems.

In IC, however, the pragmatic dimension can be problematic. An interaction can be seen from a pragmatic perspective

- on a micro level, focussing on *communicative acts*, which Wilkins ambiguously calls 'communicative functions';

- on a macro level, referring to Schmidt's (1990) *communicative moves*, which, as the name suggests, are more complex, taking chess as a metaphor for communication. As in a game of chess, there are moves which lead to a position of strength, and there are other moves which reveal weakness. *The problem is that moves do not have the same connotations in every culture.*

According to Schmidt, there are about twenty fundamental moves which, for our purposes, we can reduce to just over a dozen.

3.5.1 *Upward moves*

Attacking, dissenting, being ironic, giving orders and *interrupting* are the most delicate moves in an intercultural context.
We have already seen on the subject of negatives, that *dissenting* is a highly risky move. In many cultures it is practically forbidden and is substituted by a silent smile – which makes Europeans take a Japanese smile meaning "no" for a "yes" – with devastating consequences in a negotiation situation.
Attacking is also forbidden in many cultures – the problem is that there are occasions in which merely expressing one's own opinions, as Russians, Slavs and Israelis might do, can be seen as an attack, and thus as an aggressive move by someone wishing to obtain a dominant position.
The use of *irony* is to be avoided in an intercultural context because what to the speaker may seem like a harmless joke might be interpreted as sarcasm or even insult.
Giving orders clearly indicates a dominant position - it is an obviously risky move, and every language has forms which make it possible to avoid using the imperative, or, at least, to soften it; in English, for example, a sensitive speaker would make intensive use of *please, would, could, may,* and so on.
In a formal context, *giving orders* can be substituted by other moves such as *suggesting* or *proposing,* which treat the interlocutor (whose agreement is being sought) as being on an equal level with the speaker, and not in a position of inferiority.
The last of the strong moves, *interrupting,* is particularly difficult to

manage. On the one hand, interrupting is a feature of cultures which collaborate in communication, as we have seen in 4.2: the interrupter 'constructs' the discourse together with the person being interrupted, and does not mean to be aggressive, but rather, to work together towards a common aim. But the interruption may be viewed by many north European and American cultures as aggressive, an invasion of linguistic space, and thereby risks sparking off what in relational theory is termed an *escalation*.

3.5.2 *Downward moves*

These include *changing the subject, defending, asking for an explanation, apologising.*
In some cultures *changing the subject* is seen as a prerogative of someone who is in a dominant position, while in other cultures it is seen as an inability to continue a discussion, and changing topic becomes a means of saving face; this is a move which Arabs often resort to, to avoid admitting defeat. The problem arises when a European insists on a particular topic, and is seen as someone who wants to humiliate the interlocutor and make him lose face.
Even *defending* is a risky move, since it can be interpreted as obstinacy, if the defence is persistent.
An apparently subservient move, but one which can prove useful since it allows the user to gain time and often causes the interlocutor embarrassment, is *asking for an explanation,* but this is not usually a cause of intercultural problems.
Finally, *apologizing* is a very delicate move; an Arab prefers to avoid it altogether, so as not to lose face, and South Americans, concerned about their sense of *honra*, tend not to do it, or at least do not like being put into a position in which they have to apologize.
(The pragmatics dimension has only been referred to briefly here, but in Balboni 1999 there is an extensive bibliography for those interested in intercultural pragmatics).

4. Non-verbal codes

> a. body language: gestures, facial expressions, body odours and smells
> b. distance and contact between bodies
> c. the language of objects, clothes, and status symbols

Non-verbal codes form a closed system comprising only three components as can be seen in the icon. Three sectors of the science of communication study these codes: kinesics, proxemics, objectemics.

4.1 The fundamental role of non verbal languages in ICCC

The risks connected with the use of non-verbal languages in intercultural contexts is certainly greater than those associated with verbal language. There are two explanations for this, and they come from neurolinguistics and pragmalinguistics.

a. *we are first seen and then listened to*, the neurolinguists tell us: contextual comprehension, based on the activity of the right hemisphere of the brain, precedes verbal comprehension. This means that the information conveyed by non-verbal signs creates a pre-context for verbal information and in a way guides, facilitates or prevents verbal comprehension;

b. *we are more looked at than listened to*: about 80% of the information which reaches the brain cortex comes from sight while only about 10% comes from language. The latter of course is more sophisticated information, but as we have seen in point "a" it reaches the cortex later, and part of it may be biased by what the receiver of the message has already seen.

c. *in case of conflict, non verbal communication prevails over verbal communication*. This phenomenon is well known in

> pragmalinguistics, where a phrase (for example, 'that was clever of Paul') accompanied by a non-verbal signal, such as a wink, means the exact opposite of what has been said.

For these reasons careful attention must be paid to non-verbal elements if we are to describe or teach ICCC - and this includes the fact that the use of non verbal language is unconscious, and we pay much more attention to the verbal dimension, thereby leading to cultural conflicts in this area.

4.2. Body languages

The body is a source of much involuntary *information*, such as sweating, trembling, flushing red, etc., but it can also be used to *communicate* intentionally or to underline meanings which have been expressed through verbal language. We shall consider some of the more delicate areas of body language.

a. *smiling*
People often smile as they listen. In Europe this gesture is intended to communicate generic agreement with the speaker, or at least to indicate comprehension of what is being said; in some other cultures this is less likely to be the case. As pointed out previously, an embarrassed Japanese host, to avoid offending a foreign guest by saying 'no', may limit himself to a smile and an awkward silence; our belief that 'to be silent is to show assent' is not valid here;

b. *eyes*
In western cultures, looking the interlocutor in the eyes is usually interpreted as a sign of frankness, but in many cultures, in the far east, and in Arab countries, looking a man straight in the eyes may be considered a challenge, while looking at a woman in the same way is interpreted as sexual soliciting.
Lowered eyes, or eyes which are almost closed, suggest a lack of attention in Europe, but in Japan they may indicate respect, for example to a lecturer; they communicate complete attention, and that they listener does not wish to risk being distracted.

Raising the eyes skywards, and sometimes making a slight click of the tongue at the same time, indicates a negation in Sicily and many other Mediterranean cultures;

c. *facial expressions*
These may have a symbolic value: to express emotions, feelings, judgements and thoughts through facial mimicry is an 'obvious' thing to do in Italy or Spain, but in the far east this may not be appreciated; from an early age children are brought up to the idea of 'inscrutability', i.e. that they must not reveal their own feelings;

d. *arms and hands*
Gestures with the hands often underline or replace words, but they have different meanings according to the culture, in the same way that the lexis changes from one language to another.
Among the riskiest signs are the two which mean 'OK': a closed fist and raised thumb is considered vulgar and offensive in south-east Asia, the equivalent of the raised middle finger for an American, while the thumb and index finger joined to form an 'O' has the same interpretation (i.e. the act of sodomy) in Slav countries.
Many other signals made with the hands, and which are studied in kinesics, are risky because they can offend or mean something different;

e. *legs and feet*
In the Arab world to cross legs is to reveal the soles of ones shoes, which indicates a lack of respect; if the leg is allowed to swing back and forth, the gesture recalls a kicking movement and means 'get out of here';

f. *sweating* and *body noises*
Sweating is a natural process, but the *smell* of sweat is interpreted differently: in Europe and America if someone realizes they are sweating they feel dirty, while in other cultures the smell of sweat does not have negative connotations.
Body noises are just as delicate: blowing one's nose, sneezing, spitting, burping or farting are allowed in some cultures and forbidden in others. For example, to blow one's nose (discreetly) is allowed in western

cultures, but in the far east it is often considered disrespectful and vulgar. Similarly, burping and spitting (and sometimes intestinal rumbles) are forbidden in western cultures but tolerated in Asia and some Slav areas.

4.3 Distance between bodies

All animals live in a sort of invisible bubble which protects their intimacy and indicates their safety distance, i.e. the minimum distance needed to defend themselves or to escape from attack. For humans, this distance is about 60 cm, the length of an outstretched arm.

The 'bubble' is a natural phenomenon, while its dimensions and its role of intimacy are determined by *culture*, and so can vary; breaking the rules of proxemics, the grammar which governs interpersonal distances, can be seen as an aggression.

On the European coast of the Mediterranean, coming closer than arm's length to someone means invading their territory, but for northern Europeans the distance needs to be doubled. On the other side of the Mediterranean, in the Arab world, the distance is much shorter, to the point of non-existence, and speakers can touch each other's chest as an indication of the truthfulness of what they are saying; they are literally speaking with 'their hearts in their hands'.

In south-east Asia and in many Islamic areas it is forbidden to place one's hand on a child's head, since heads are taboo - but the gesture is a common one for Italians who wish to express simple affection for a child.

4.4. Clothes and other objects

The biggest problems are of a religious nature, or concern formality, and the showing off of wealth or status.

a. *religious problems*
Religious problems are exemplified by the wearing of the Islamic veil or chador, or the dagger carried by Sikhs, which led to difficulties in

Great Britain. It is religion which imposes followers to cover up all parts of their body except for head and hands, whatever the temperature.

Another problem concerns dress code, or formality: for example, in the United States people who are in professional contact with the public should wear dark clothes, while in Europe lighter colours and patterns are possible. In contrast, in the USA and in South America a tie can be all that is needed to indicate formality in a work environment, whereas in Europe, especially in the south, a jacket and tie are needed, and shirts should have long sleeves;

b. *formality*

In an invitation, the way in which the degree of formality required is communicated may be complex; for example, the Italian formula *è gradito l'abito scuro* ('dark dress would be appreciated') indicates a level of formality far beyond the colour of the clothes.

Women dripping jewellery, people who carry several mobile phones, the use of chauffeur-driven company cars can all be examples of exhibitionism for an Italian, but in many cultures in emerging countries they are a way of indicating socio-economic status. In some European contexts the effect may be that the interlocutor is considered a nouveau riche boor, who does not understand how 'evolved' society functions. The European thus adopts a position of superiority, leading inevitably to resentment on the part of the interlocutor.

5. Cultural values affecting communication

> *Fundamental cultural values:*
>
> a. space and time
> b. public/private
> c. hierarchy, status, respect
> d. family
> e. loyalty, fair play
> f. etc.

Much of the literature on intercultural communication is of an anthropological or sociological nature; in some cases, as for example with the mass of materials on this theme produced by the Council of Europe, there is also a politico-cultural dimension, inspired by an idea of 'intercultural citizenship'. But although intercultural 'communication' is frequently referred to in the literature, the communicative dimension tends to be somewhat peripheral; whereas, in our approach, it is the centre around which the whole model revolves, the entire system of analysis and description of ICCC. Within this strictly communicative perspective, however, cultural values, which form the nucleus of the 'software of the mind', are also fundamental.

Unlike verbal and non-verbal codes, which, are closed systems, cultural values form an open set (and for this reason the list in the icon concludes with *etc.*).

The components which we shall deal with have been chosen on the basis of the consequences they can have on a communicational and relational level in a range of communicative events; the relation between cultural values and events is indicated in the diagram in chapter 2 by an arrow pointing in both directions.

For example, in defining the ICCC needed by teachers when dealing with immigrant students, it is of paramount importance to be aware

- that Muslim cultures (including those in 'lay' Muslim countries such as Turkey) have a quite different idea of "knowledge" from the one commonly held in Western cultures;
- that in many Asian cultures the teacher is supposed to be

right *per se* and has a high status, so if a student has not understood something they will never ask the teacher to repeat what he or she has said;
- that in other cultures (e.g. Rom and Sinti cultures) a teacher is respected if he or she shows hierarchical status by moving students around the room without giving any reason for doing so, or by administering corporal punishment (or simulating it), to students who make mistakes or do not obey,
- *etcetera*.

"Etcetera" is in italics because the cultural values which a teacher working with immigrants will come into contact with form an 'open set', and every open set, by definition, end with *etc.*
In other words, the cultural values which one has to be aware of to be 'competent' in intercultural communication change according to ones role as an international manager, a diplomat, a UN peacekeeper, a functionary in an NGO working in an international context, a teacher working with immigrant children, *etc.*

5.1 The concept of time

Imagine a photo seen thousands of times in a tourist brochure, TV documentaries, and perhaps even taken by ourselves: it shows a row of sand dunes stretching towards the horizon, and a set of footprints coming from who knows where and disappearing into the distance. What sense of space and time can be derived from someone from an Arab culture, rooted in the image of a boundless desert, where space just crossed is no different from space about to be crossed, where time is marked out not by a succession of villages, towns, or woods, but simply by the progress of the sun through the sky?
We shall return to the concept of space in 5.2. For the moment let us consider that of time.
It should not come as a surprise if a people used to the desert day and the lunar calendar - which means that the start of Ramadan is brought forward by eleven days each year - is not punctual or reliable in its organisation of time in the same way as Americans or Europeans, who

have been brought up to an idea of time as something fixed, permanently in harness with festivals which mark out the year: a white Christmas, flowers in bloom at Easter, August bank holiday in the heat, and falling leaves on All Souls Day...

This different conception of time, which Thais refer to as 'elastic', in contrast with the 'string' conception of time typical of Europeans, leads to relational, rather than communicative, problems, but we refer to it here to point out that some notions which might appear to be natural (such as the cyclical nature of time) in actual fact have a cultural dimension.

But there are also communicative problems related to the concept of time:

a. *structured time*
The agenda for a meeting connects contents in temporal succession; for people from Mediterranean cultures there is no problem in starting with point 3, which can be dealt with rapidly, move on to point 1, postpone point 2 to the end of the meeting if there is time for it, and to deal with points 4 and 5 together. This is normal praxis, and extremely efficient, because flexible; but for a northern European or an American an agenda is fixed and sacrosanct, and people get irritated – and make aggressive moves as a result – when faced with Mediterranean 'chaos';

b. *time as personal space*
Turn taking is seen by many cultures as belonging to personal space; someone who interrupts is thus invading space. In a meeting in which each participant is expected to take turns, one after the other, following a strict order, it is important to wait one's turn. But people from Latin cultures do not do this; they consider that what they have to say is sufficiently important to justify interrupting the order, but in so doing they irritate their north European or north American interlocutors, who feel under attack (a feeling which may have been confirmed by a raised voice, or over gesticulation), and reply accordingly...

c. *empty time: silence.*
For a Scandinavian, silence, even prolonged silence, at a meeting is acceptable, but for someone from a Latin culture it is unthinkable. To

avoid silence, small talk is preferred. But this is risky, since topics which are neutral or agreeable in one culture may be taboo or inappropriate in another.

5.2 Public/private space

Let us to return to the image of the desert in 5.1 (which we have borrowed from Della Puppa 2005).
Should we be surprised if an Arab considers open space as belonging to everyone and no-one – a *res nullius* where one can leave rubbish without batting an eyelid provoking scandal for the north European or north American who considers that space which belongs to everyone is therefore his, and personal, and thus has to be defended, looked after, and kept clean?
Should we be surprised if in the Arab world and in many Mediterranean towns the façades of houses have peeling paintwork and the streets are dirty and full of rubbish, while private space – the patio and the inside of the house – is clean and tidy?
Here again the problems are not strictly communicative, but our intention is to point out the culture-bound, not natural, origin of certain behaviour patterns.
But there are also communicative problems related to space, since, as we have seen, many cultures consider personal space to be sacred and inviolable, even at a meeting or during group work: the southern European who occupies another person's space is an 'invader' and the north European or north American interlocutor, who feels under attack, replies with aggressive communicative moves, which are not understood by the Italian, Greek or Spaniard, thereby sparking off the communicative escalation we spoke of in 3.5.

5.3 Hierarchy, status, respect

These are three aspects of the same phenomenon, namely social differentiation and the cultural necessity to organize communication between different levels.

5.3.1 *Hierarchy and status*

There are *explicit* and *implicit* hierarchies: the first is made evident by signs, which may range from the size and position of an armchair in an office, to the stripes on a soldier's uniform; the second is governed by understatement, making it difficult for an outsider to work out the actual hierarchy, with the risk that he or she may select the wrong person as interlocutor. For example, the official head of a Chinese delegation is often the most elderly (since age confers status in the Far East), but this person may not necessarily have the decisional power; conversely, in China, an alphabetical list of European delegates is likely to be considered hierarchically since alphabetical order is not used.
There are also *permeable* and *impermeable* hierarchies.
In the first case, communication is possible even across hierarchical divides – to take an extreme example, a porter can pass on an idea to the CEO of a company. Other hierarchies are impermeable, meaning that all communication has to follow a strict hierarchical order, moving from one level to the next, with the risk that the porter's idea may never reach the CEO, or if it does, it may be presented as someone else's.
Signs indicating hierarchy are of various types - from uniforms and furniture to the number of bows or the way a present is wrapped, as in Japan. Depending on the type of communicative event, and the context - commercial, diplomatic, military, etc. - knowledge of those signs indicating status and hierarchy is an essential component of ICCC.

5.3.2 *Respect*

Hierarchy and status determine the degree of respect due to the interlocutor.
Respect can take various forms: kinesic (bows and body movements), proxemic (distance from the most important person), and linguistic.
In Romance and Germanic languages, as well as in Arabic and Chinese, there is pronominal differentiation to indicate a friendly relationship and a more respectful one, but in English, today's lingua franca, there is only the pronoun *you*, making it necessary to indicate respect through the use of modal verbs such as *could* and *would*, and other linguistic forms.

In recent decades the delicate communicative nature of forms of respect had led to the use of *politically correct* terminology:
- *negro* has become *black*;
- the opposition between *Mr* (a term which does not reveal marital status) and *Mrs/Miss* has been replaced by *Mr/Ms*;
- there are problems with the use of titles (*chairman/chairwoman/chairperson*, in English, for example) in languages which have female forms of the same words;
- many socially humble jobs have been redescribed, for example, dustmen are now in some cultures 'ecological operators', the servant became 'a domestic' and is now a 'family collaborator' in Italy, and so on;
- in the same way, physical handicaps have been redescribed, so that the blind are now called 'non-seeing person' in many cultures, while 'disabled', to avoid the negative implications of the *dis* prefix, have become 'differently able'.
Dozens of similar examples can be found if we refer to ethnic groups, race, religion, sexuality, etc.
With these examples we believe we have clarified the fact that the socio-pragmatic component of ICCC can only be mastered if the appropriate forms of respect are mastered, and that these count far more than grammatical correctness and lexical precision for communicative purposes.

5.4 The concept of family

This is connected to the problem of respect, since in almost all cultures a degree of respect is due to a member of the family of the interlocutor. The problem comes from the fact that the idea of family changes greatly from one culture to another.
For the mafia, a family includes dozens of real families; for a Japanese businessman the company is very similar a family, with the result that criticism of the company is like a personal affront; for a German the state is a large family, and so political irony – especially if it comes from a foreigner – is not appreciated, just as the British, who may criticize and deride the royal family themselves, won't tolerate others doing so if they are not subjects of Her Majesty, the 'Mother' of all her people.

5.5 Honesty, loyalty, fair play

In the common European perception of things, middle Eastern and South American civil servants are corrupt, but locals see things differently: since salaries are small, what we see as 'corruption' is often a sort of 'productivity bonus', so that the official preparing a document believes he has the right to ask for a tip, in other words a payment related to the importance of the document, and the speed with which it is produced...

Similarly, the Japanese worker who criticises his company – even if the criticism is justifiable and concrete – is seen as disloyal.

These differences of perception have major consequences which are not only relational (which is obvious) but also communicative, since they lead to the use of wrong communicative moves, often aggressive, or else they may become the object of small talk, which southern Europeans use to fill up silences in a meeting (see 5.1.b) in the belief that this is insignificant, but which can be seen negatively by their interlocutors.

6. Communicative events

a. cocktails and dinners
b. telephone calls
c. negotiations
d. public speech
e. group work
f. classroom lesson
g. etc.

Many of the examples we have given in previous chapters refer more or less explicitly to specific communicative events. In this chapter we need refer to only a few communicative problems which are typical of some communicative events.

We should first recall that a 'communicative event', in terms of the ethnomethodology of communication, is a social event, requiring the presence of more than one participant (and some of whom may not be physically present: for example, a political leader speaking to a journalist is actually communicating with his political adversaries, his allies, and millions of viewers who may or may not vote for him), whose aims may be more or less concealed, who make communicative moves, and whose linguistic acts are codified by well established norms.

The most widely known model of analysis of the communicative event if provided by Hymes (1972).

6.1 Cocktails and dinners

This is a very common event, in which communication has a primary role – beyond the cultural choice of food, related to the religion of the participants, or the philosophical choices (such as vegetarianism). The main problems concern:

> *a.* the formality of clothes and the way to communicate the level of formality in the invitation card; an Italian invitation reads *è gradito l'abito scuro* ('dark clothes appreciated'), which has nothing to do with the colour of the clothes, but indicates a high level of formality;

b. the way to communicate *the beginning and the end* of the cocktail: an American invitation card may read, after the date, "from 6 to 8", meaning that at 8 o' clock the cocktail will be over and that guests should have left by this time – while in a southern European or South American culture the moment of leaving has negative connotations; the guest who leaves early draws attention to himself. In these cultures, it is better to stay on late, following the rules of a Greek *symposium;*

c. the way to communicate the *beginning* of the meal: in some cultures the host begins to eat first, in others, it is the hostess who takes her seat at table who gives the signal to start, in still others there are formulaic expressions such as *bon appétit*, which people, again from other cultures, think are in bad taste;

d. *topics* for conversation: in many cultures, only informal conversation is allowed, and it is forbidden to speak of business, whereas in other cultures this is perfectly acceptable;

e. the way to *communicate with waiting staff*, how to say 'please' and 'thank you' for their services.

6.2 Telephone conversations

The main problem with this type of event lies in the cost of intercontinental phone calls and the use or misuse made of the interlocutor's personal time. There are two opposing views:

- the American view, common among Western businessmen, that *time is money;*
- the Oriental and Southern European tradition, which requires a series of polite exchanges, and which, in the case of someone from the Far East, may last for several minutes, with references to health, family, etc.

Thus the American sees Japanese politeness as showing lack of respect towards the costs the American has to bear, and the Japanese businessman sees the American telephone call as an unpleasant event in which there is no room for the rules of polite society.

6.3 Negotiation

Negotiation strategies constitute a specific field in pyscho-pragmatic relational and transactional research, and so do not come under the ICCC heading.

From our strictly communicative point of view, it is not just the various kinesic and proxemic components, and the choice of communicative moves, (which we have referred to above) which have an important role in negotiation, but also the textual structure which changes according to the culture of origin (cf 3.1).

Whereas it is relatively easy to be careful about one's tone of voice, the use of one's hands, etc., it is much more difficult to restructure one's thoughts, since textual form and structure provides the framework for the complex cognitive form.

6.4 Group work

This is one of the most common events involving people from different cultures and ICCC thus has an important role to play. Group work can be divided into four phases, in which ICCC has different functions:

a. the first phase is known as the 'chaos phase' and may last only a few seconds - but the successful conclusion of the work is dependent on it. It is the phase in which participants 'fight' for the role of leader and counter-leader, both of which are essential in a properly functioning group which needs a leader but which must not meekly accept all decisions made by the leader; if we recall the problems related to hierarchical structures (cf. 5.3) and the signals which indicate them, respect, political correctness, etc., it is easy to realize that this 'fight' (often fought with non-verbal codes, with just a few apparently insignificant spoken exchanges) is highly delicate on an inter-cultural level;

b. the second phase involves *assigning roles* and *agreeing work procedures;* the only other communicative problems are the normal ones associated with an intercultural conversation;

c. the third phase may last hours, days, or even weeks. It is the *actual work* phase, and success depends on being able to control the communicative moves it entails;

d. the fourth phase is the presentation of the results; if it is a written presentation, the American text-structure model we have already referred to is likely to be chosen; if the presentation is an oral one (or written and oral), the communicative problems are likely to be greater (cf. 6.4).

6.5 Speaking in public

Presenting the results of group work, delivering a lecture, making a formal toast, and so on, are examples of speaking in public. Particularly problematic are

a. the choice of 'psychological and relational key' (to use Hymes' 1972 parameter); for example, a choice to make a formal presentation requires appropriate syntax and lexis; but the 'key' may be misunderstood by people from different cultures who may view a formal style as superiority or informality as shoddiness;

b. the presentation of the speaker to the audience can cause problems: for example, Americans tend to underline the many qualities and achievements of the speaker, embarrassing Europeans who prefer understatement and brevity; in contrast, an American speaker may feel that he or she has not been properly appreciated in a presentation made by a European;

c. the beginning of a speech, a lecture, or a formal toast requires an opening joke in the United States, but this may seem out of place to Europeans;

d. in the discussion phases the major intercultural problem lies in the choice of communicative moves.

6.6 The lesson

This is a specific communicative event in which speaking in public, conversation, negotiation, group work, presentation of results, etc., intermingle.

In schools and universities the number of students from cultures different from the dominant culture is continually increasing, both as a result of migration (often linked to poverty, but in some cases to the movement of high level professionals), and by the ever more popular choice of studying abroad. If there is no awareness of the problems of intercultural communicative problems and the necessary communicative strategies are not adopted, the result is often the *negation of communication:* the foreign student remains silent and does not communicate, not because he doesn't understand the language, but especially because the rules of communication in such a complex event as a lesson are not clear.

The international complexity of the lessons is often undervalued by the student himself, as well as by the teachers, all of whom are convinced that the problems are simply of a linguistic nature.

In our view, all intercultural citizenship projects are destined to fail if they do not take into account intercultural communication as well as linguistic communication. (The Venice school has given ample attention to this problem: Luise 2003, Santipolo *et al* 2003, Pavan 2004, Triolo 2004, Caon 2005, Celentin and Cognigni 2005, Della Puppa 2006, D'Annunzio 2006).

7. Constructing Intercultural Communicative Competence

We have chosen the phrase 'constructing competences' to be coherent with our affirmation at the beginning of this *Document*: descriptions cannot be taught or learnt, but models can; and ICCC as presented here is a model, which can be filled with contents following a logic of lifelong learning. But there are two other reasons for doing so, and they are exquisitely pedagogical:

> *a. the verb 'construct' focuses on the process, not the means*; whether competence is achieved through autonomous learning based on the model and filled with the experiences of the individual learner, or whether it is taught by a teacher in the controlled environment of a school, a company, the military, etc., is irrelevant;
>
> *b.* the word recalls constructivist methodology, which holds that *knowledge is not imparted* by someone who has it to someone who hasn't, *but is constructed together*, through dialogue and shared experience, following a conceptual framework - in other words, the model which we have outlined.

In this final chapter we shall see how our reflection on ICCC, so far viewed from semiotic, ethnomethodological and pragmatic perspectives, can also be seen quite naturally in a context of language teaching methodology, which is the focus of study of the Venice group, and whose position these documents illustrate (besides the works cited in 6.5, see also Balboni 1999 and 2004; Pavan 2002, 2003, 2004a, 2004b, Della Puppa 2004, Caon and D'Annunzio 2006, Luise 2006).

7.1 ICCC constructed by adult students

By 'adult' we mean people who have acquired experience (not just a legal definition of the term), and who have decided of their own accord to begin a programme of intercultural awareness, who are responsible for what they learn, and who view the teacher as a social peer who has a dual competence, both in methodology and contents.

In this case the teacher's role is simple:

> a. to *elicit* the student's experience, to use this as a starting point: training in ICCC begins with systematic reflection on one's own experiences of intercultural contacts (whether first hand, or seen in films, read in books, recounted by colleagues);
> b. to *lead* students to grasp the four basic components of the model (the four icons in the table in chapter 2);
> c. to *facilitate the discovery* of the components which comprise the four icons, where this is possible, or merely to *list and explain* them if they do not emerge from a groups construction;
> d. to *co-ordinate* the group as they insert contents into each category, whether these are of a general nature ("to *attack* is one of the most delicate moves in CCIC") or specific: ("The Chinese are physically repulsed by the Westerner who blows his nose and puts his handkerchief in his pocket; similarly, a Westerner has the same reaction when he see sees a Chinese person spitting in public");
> e. to *supply information*, through anecdotes, bibliographies, film sequences, and so on, to complete the picture;
> f. to *lead students to a concluding reflection* about specific values or problems, and about ICCC; this means empowering students with the model, so that for the rest of their lives they will be able to perfect, adapt, or renew its contents;
> g. *to provide a methodology* for the above, i.e. the life-long and life-wide continuation of the work of analyzing and describing ICCC.

An effective tool for point (g) above, and which can be used throughout the course, is a simple data bank, which each student can compile (either in a ring binder, or on a computer file), listing the headings from each icon:

Underlying cultural values:
a   time and space
b   public/private
c   hierarchy, status, respect

d family (including extended family)
e loyalty and fair play
f etc.

Verbal codes:
a sound
b choice of words
c grammar problems
d text structure
e socio-pragmatic aspects

Non-verbal codes:
a expressions, gestures, body odours and noises
b distance between bodies
c objects, clothes, and status symbols

Communicative events:
a cocktails and dinners
b telephone calls
c group work
d speaking in public
e negotiating
f etc.

Individual headings may be better organized with sub-headings which can be derived from the sections in which we have described each element: for example, 'gestures' can be defined as

- gesturing with the head (movements of the head, eyes, mouth, expresssions)
- gesturing with the hands and the arms
- gesturing with the legs and the feet
- etc.

Like the course itself, a databank can have two aspects, since it can have two different objectives:

a. to explore ICCC *within two cultures,* for example 'problems of intercultural communication between Turks and Italians'; or, in a wider context, 'problems of intercultural communication between Latin Europeans and Germanic Europeans';

b. *cultural pluralism*, following a model which could be of interest to many multinational companies, diplomatic corps, academics and the armed forces; the file would have a vertical axis with the above list, and a horizontal axis listing countries and/or cultures; a simple click would open a *word* document with all the information gathered on that specific country or culture, and which may include videos, photos, links, and other material exemplifying and illustrating a specific intercultural problem. Of course this would be a 'file progress'.

As can be seen, the philosophy behind a training course to construct ICCC is highly co-operative; such a course need not last a long time, only the time it takes to make students aware of the problem, by presenting a model, and teaching them how to use it and complete it during their life time:

> *students can be taught to observe ICCC,*
> *but ICCC itself cannot be taught.*

7.2 ICCC in a foreign language course other than English

The underlying philosophy does not change, compared with that described in 7.1, but the methodology and time scale change.

We should first clarify that by 'foreign language course' we mean both a normal school course, and a course for a company; the ages of students and their levels of motivation change, but the formal structure remains the same. A course in a foreign language is also a course in language and *area studies*, as the American *Army Specialized Training Program* during the second world war defined its work on the culture and civilization of the people, or peoples, who used that language. In many countries, university chairs in languages are called chairs in the 'language and culture' (of French, Russian, etc) rather than just 'language'.

Usually this term is meant in a restrictive sense; cultural elements are taught when they illustrate a 'way of life', and are useful from a socio-pragmatic point of view to communicate in the foreign language, but non-verbal languages and values - the *softwares of the mind* - are ignored, or at most, offered only sporadically, in a non-systematic way.

In a wider LTM context students would create a file (hard copy or electronic) such as the one described in 7.1: in this way it becomes possible to teach how to watch a film, gather and record information throughout and beyond the school curriculum: *non scholae, sed vita, discimus*.

7.3 ICCC in course of English as a second or foreign language

In this context the problem becomes more complex, since English is the first language in the UK and Ireland, the United States, and other countries, and is the second language in many parts of the so-called *English-speaking world* from India to Nigeria and South Africa, in areas such as Scandinavia, and is the language of globalisation, used for commercial, tourist, and military purposes, etc.

This means that the ICCC model must be proposed, and its use should be taught

    a. in relation to mother tongue English cultures, at least in the two major areas (British/European and American), by exploring its values, by studying the use of non-verbal languages, the cultural rules underlying the main events, etc.;

    b. in relation to the rest of the world, both where English is a second language, and where it is used only as a lingua franca.

This second point indicates a fundamental shift in the teaching of culture in the English language class, still limited to point (a), and, especially in Europe, a single aspect of (a): British culture, i.e., England, with just a few nods in the direction of the Celtic fringe, Scotland, Ireland and Wales.

References

The list below is not a complete bibliography, but simply a list of the studies explicitly quoted in this essay. As in other volumes in the series, all the relevant work done in the field by members of the Venice group is included.

ATTARD P. A. (ed.), 1996, *Language and Culture Awareness in Language Learning/ Teaching for the Development of Learner Autonomy*, Strasbourg, CoE - CCC.

BALBONI P. E., 1999, *Parole comuni, culture diverse. Guida alla comprensione interculturale, [Common Words, Different Cultures. A Guide to Intercultural Understanding]* Venice, Marsilio.

BALBONI P. E., 2004, "La comunicazione interculturale nella classe con immigrati", ["Intercultural communication in classes with immigrant pupils] in M. FIORUCCI (a cura di.), *Incontri. Spazi e luoghi della mediazione interculturale, [Meeting Points. The Spatial Context o Iintercultural Mediation]* Roma, Armando, 2004.

BEGOTTI P., 2006, *Insegnare italiano all'immigrato adulto, [Teaching Italian to Adult Immigrants]* Perugia, Guerra.

BYRAM M., 1997, *Teaching and Assessing Intercultural Communicative Competence*, London, Multilingual Matters.

BYRAM M., BEACCO J. C., 2003, *Guide pour l'élaboration des politiques linguistiques éducatives en Europe*, Strasbourg, CoE.

BYRAM M., ZARATE G., 1996, *Les jeunes confrontés à la différence*, Strasbourg, CoE.

CAON F., 2005, *Un approccio umanistico-affettivo all'insegnamento dell'italiano a non nativi, [A Humanist/Affective Approach to the Teaching of Italian to Non Natives]* Venezia, Cafoscarina.

CAON F., D'ANNUNZIO B., 2006, *Il laboratorio linguistico d'italiano L2*, *[The Italian L2 Laboratory]* Perugia, Guerra.

D'ANNUNZIO B., 2006, *Lo studente di origine cinese, [Students of Chinese Origin]* Perugia, Guerra.

DELLA PUPPA F., "Leggere, scrivere e far di conto. Il rapporto col sapere visto dalla parte degli allievi stranieri". ["Reading, writing and counting- how foreign pupils approach learning"] In C. GREZZI – F. GUERINI – P. MULINELLI (a cura di), *Italiano e lingue immigrate a confronto: riflessioni per la pratica didattica*, *[Italian and ImmigrantLlanguages Compared: Reflections for Teaching]* Perugia, Guerra.

DELLA PUPPA F., 2005, *Lo studente di origine araba, [Students from Arab Speaking Countries]* Perugia, Guerra.

CELENTIN P., COGNIGNI E., 2005, *Lo studente di origine slava, [Students from Slavic Speaking Countries]* Perugia, Guerra.

GANNON M. J., 1994, *Understanding Global Cultures. Metaphorical Journeys through 17 Countries,* S. Francisco, Sage.

HOFSTEDE G., 1991, *Cultures and Organizations: Software of the Mind,* London, McGraw-Hill.

LANGACKER, R. W. 1990, *Concept, Image and Symbol. The Cognitive Basis of Grammar,* Berlino, Mouton.

LEGRENZI P., 2002, *Prima lezione di scienze cognitive, [A First Lesson in Cognitive Sciences]* Bari, Laterza.

LUISE M.C. (a cura di), 2003, *Italiano Lingua Seconda: fondamenti e metodi, [Italian as a Second Language]* Perugia, Guerra.

LUISE M.C., 2006, *Insegnare l'italiano a immigrati, [Teaching Italian to Immigrants]* Torino UTETUniversità.

HYMES D., 1972, "Models of Interaction of Language and Social Life", in J.J.GUMPERS and D.HYMES (eds.), *Directions in Sociolinguistics: the Ethnography of Communication,* New York, Holt, Rinehart & Winston.

PAVAN E., 2002, "Cultura e comunicazione non verbale nell'insegnamento delle lingue straniere", ["Culture and non verbal communication in foreign language teaching"] in *Scuola e Lingue Moderne*, Milano, Garzanti, n° 4.

PAVAN E., 2003, "La cultura e la civiltà italiane e il loro insegnamento in una prospettiva interculturale", "The teaching of Italian culture and civilisation in an intercultural perspective" DOLCI R. e CELENTIN, P. (a cura di), 2003, *La formazione di base del docente di italiano per stranieri, [Initial Training of Teachers of Italian as a Foreign Language]* Roma, Bonacci.

PAVAN E., 2004a, "Cinema e comunicazione interculturale", [Cinema and intercultural communication] *Scuola e Lingue Moderne*, Milano, Garzanti, n° 7-8.

PAVAN E., 2004b, "Cultura e civiltà nella classe di lingue", [Culture and civilisation in the laanguage classs] in SERRAGIOTTO G. (a cura di), *Le lingue straniere nella scuola, [Foreign Languages in Schools]* Torino, UTET Libreria.

SANTIPOLO M., TOSINI M. e TUCCIARONE S., 2003, *Introduzione alla comunicazione interculturale in ambito socio-sanitario, [An Introduction to Intercultural Communication in the Health Services]* Venezia, UIL-FPL Veneto.

SCHMIDT E., 1990, *Comunicare nelle organizzazioni. La teoria sistemica della comunicazione nella formazione aziendale, [Communication in Organsiations. The Systemic Theory of Communication in Company Training Programmes]* Milano, Unicopli.

TRIOLO R., 2004, *Vedere gli immigrati attraverso il cinema, [The Portrayal of Immigrants in the Cinema]* Perugia, Guerra.